T0146978

The
PFC

D . A . WELLS

authorHOUSE®

AuthorHouse™
1663 Liberty Drive
Bloomington, IN 47403
www.authorhouse.com
Phone: 1 (800) 839-8640

Published by AuthorHouse 09/26/2019

ISBN: 978-1-7283-2905-5 (sc)
ISBN: 978-1-7283-2904-8 (e)

Print information available on the last page.

This book is printed on acid-free paper.

Dedication and Credits

To my daughter Susanne for typing and editing my book, excellent job.

To my friend Joan at the YMCA where I met her, for encouraging me to write the book, I bet she will be surprised.

Also for my dear friend Kay who encouraged me and offered valuable suggestions while writing the book.

And finally, for all those I spoke to about the book who want a copy to read, my fans.

Thank you all,
D. A. WELLS

Preface

By D. A. Wells

July 7, 2019

One has to wonder sometimes, why we do some things we wish later we could erase every bad memory.

After my wife Lois died in 2008, several months of mourning and seeing all the work not getting done, even the most basic, I finally kicked myself in the butt to get going and put things in order.

About a year later I decided to join the "Silver Sneakers" at the YMCA that my health insurance agent suggested. Preventative medicine. When I entered the Y one morning to sign up, I discovered a few friends I had not seen in close to thirty years were there. I also made some new friends including a woman I called Joanie (her name was Joan) who wrote articles for a local newspaper. I read some of her articles and may have mentioned that in high school an English teacher said I should write short stories and poems. I never did anything with that, I wasn't interested then. She said I should write a book and my response was, "What should I write about?" Well, she said, "If you don't try you will never know if you can." After thinking about it I concluded I could only write about my experiences and settled on the two years I was in the Army. Many strange things occurred that may be of interest as well as a few laughs. I was able to remember a lot more than I thought so I hope you enjoy it.

Chapter I

DRAFTED

Brother was that ever an experience in the Army. Anyone who was in the service can relate to what I am about to tell you, well maybe not everything as you will see later.

When you begin "Basic Training", the first thing you learn is you have one right – to do as you are told. Right guys? Let's back up a minute – when you are inducted, and me being a shy guy, we had to strip down buck naked (about twenty guys) for a physical. They checked our teeth, our heads for lice and the finale was bend over and spread your wings while a doctor walked by about five feet away from us and checked for 'who knows what'.

Lastly, each of us were taken to an office where some guy asked us questions privately. His first question, which I thought was a dumb one being a naive guy, was "Do you like girls?" I was puzzled. I think I said "of course". We later found out he was a phycologist. Before entering the service I did not know what a homosexual was. Sure my buddies and I used some of the references to them but did not know what they meant.

From the Milwaukee induction center we were taken by an Army bus to Fort Sheridan, Illinois where we were given clothes too large, but at least the boots and shoes fit. Later in Basic Training I discovered why the oversized clothes. I gained 22 pounds and filled them in.

In our group from Milwaukee was a skinny guy named Frankie who actually wanted to get in the Army. He weighed 99 pounds, the minimum required. Sometimes you hear about some fellows who are really gung ho to join the Army to get in a war. Most men in their right mind prefer not to get in combat and risk getting killed, but when called up, you go and do your duty because you have to. Some men have said if you assume you are dead, it eases the fear of being killed. Referring back to Frankie, I think he may have gained three to five pounds max, from what I heard.

From Fort Sheridan, a few days later an Army bus took us to O'Hare International Airport where we were flown by a DC-3 to Washington D.C. While on the flight we could walk around so I went to the cockpit, looked around at all the gauges surrounding the pilot and copilot and asked them how they could keep track of all those gauges. They told me it was not necessary. The only ones they needed to watch were altitude, speed, oil and fuel. While traveling on our way to Washington D.C., the plane suddenly dropped about 1,000 feet, our pilot said, which scared the hell out of us! I don't remember why they said it happens, but I guess it doesn't happen too often. After landing in D.C. we were taken by another Army bus to Fort Lee, Virginia (it's in my orders which I still have). Now I noticed it is Fort Lee, New Jersey – when did that change?

Chapter II

BASIC TRAINING

We began Basic Training on Monday morning at 5:00 A.M.…never had to get up that early before. After a few days I had black eyes because we got so little sleep (five hours or less). Our platoon sergeant was Thornhill and I will always remember him because I was the guy in this platoon whom he chose to harass the most to keep the rest of the guys in line. Well, when I realized that I goaded him to take a swing at me which would have gotten him court-martialed. When he caught on, he backed off and left me alone.

Well, our first day we had to memorize the ten general orders and your U.S. I.D. number. There was an eleventh general order to remember the first ten. It took me years to forget those first ten and purposely walk out of marching step. Brother, this is one for the books. Some of us noticed our hillbilly from the Ozarks was not taking any showers so we told him he needs to take a shower each morning like the rest of us. He still did not do it, so a few of us escorted him to the shower and gave him one with a stiff brush with his clothes on. Then we stripped him down naked and gave him another shower. You would think after that he would get the message. Nope, he still would not do it!

In Basic Training you are harassed and worked to death so you are prepared for combat, in my case the 'Korean Police Action", and the language the cadre used on us I cannot repeat here. During Basic Training we were given a series of tests to see where we fit in for the Army's purpose. All but two men who passed the

O.C.S. test (Officer's Candidate School) turned it down because we had heard that "ninety-day wonders" leading a platoon were too green for combat to lead, getting themselves killed. We figured getting a battlefield commission after learning how to stay alive would be a better way to go. One of the two who wanted to go was rejected because he could not qualify physically (too fat) so only one man went to O.C.S.

From day to day in Basic Training we have different things to learn, especially about your assigned rifle. First we learned to take it completely apart and put it back together, not only in daylight but when it was so dark you could not see anything! You had to take it apart and put it back together by feel. Then comes the day we went to the shooting range. Oh! One important thing – NEVER refer to your rifle as a gun! First you learn to handle your weapon safely. Keep your trigger finger away from the trigger. Second, never, never point your rifle at anyone, no matter if you think it's not loaded (except for the enemy of course); either straight up or preferably in a down position. Well, wouldn't you know, before we could begin shooting at targets (I bet you can guess) one of our company screw-ups loaded his weapon, gets up from his prone position (on your belly) because he has a problem, swings his rifle around and had everyone dropping to the ground, yelling for him to lower his rifle down toward the ground. After that incident I hope he was never allowed to handle any weapon again. He was more dangerous than the enemy!

After everyone settled down we began, when instructed, to shoot at targets at different distances. Well, I fired a few rounds and did not even hit the target. I was sure I was not shooting blanks. I called the sergeant over and told him what happened. He took the rifle, fired a few shots, then adjusted the sight and fired a couple more shots. Then he said, "Ok, try it now." I fired five shots, a bullseye every time - what a difference a sight makes!

Another example of 'why safety'. Whenever we had guard duty you had a loaded rifle. One evening a soldier who had already served twice in Korea and earned medals, offered to fill in for the regular drivers who did the run, but could not do it that evening. Well, at one pickup, the guard was running to the truck and trying to unload his rifle at the same time – a major no-no. It fired a shot, a 45 caliber bullet which flew through the back of the one and a half ton truck, missing the other guards, flies through the plastic window and goes into the head of our war hero – killing him instantly. He had just been waiting for his orders to muster out and go home. I don't know what happened to the dumbbell who shot him, but his sentence should have been severe.

The M1's we were using in Basic Training were used in WWII and the rifling was pitted and well worn. I was surprised you could still hit targets with them. The distances of our targets at the shooting range were 100 yards, 200 yards and 300 yards. At 300 yards and no scope, the bullseye was the size of a period at the end of a sentence.

During the eight weeks we were in Basic Training we were finally allowed to roam the camp after our training day ended. I went to the U.S.O. club I had heard about and found the music room where a piano was waiting for me to play it. (I had taken piano lessons a few years before and will tell that story in another book if this one is successful.) One of the things I wanted to do was learn to play other instruments besides the piano. Another G.I. who had been here for a few weeks longer than me said you will have to say you know how to play whichever instrument you choose. I spoke to the hostess at the U.S.O. and asked for a trumpet (at home I had a beat up cornet I played by ear which is similar to a trumpet). After some experimenting with the valves, I was able to play it fairly well, however your lips would get numb at first and I already knew not to let your cheeks expand when playing. Next I asked for a bass fiddle so I could learn to play it. It was easier than I thought. It certainly helped to know how to play the piano and I was never asked if I played any of the instruments. Anyway, another G.I. came in with his instrument and asked if he could join me. I said, "Sure." Soon a few more guys came in with their instruments to join us and we had what is called a jam session.

Later the U.S.O. hostess came in and said some people out where the dance floor was were asking if we could come out there and play so they could hear us better and dance. We did, and after about an hour about 200 people were dancing to our group (around 2:00 P.M.). By the way, we did not have any sheet music to read and the five of us played by ear. If we knew the melody, that's all it took. How often do you have five people who did not know each other and had never practiced together, who could play together like a practiced band?! I never knew their names nor saw them again after that evening.

We and two other companies were slated to go to Japan for further training prior to going to Korea. (I am getting ahead of myself again.) While nearing the end of Basic Training we had to spend a few days out in the field, very primitive. This was going to be the cadres (our trainers) against the trainees. I guess to show us how dumb we were – not ready for combat. We had heard about previous trainees being captured by the cadre at night, catching them off guard. Well, we were not going to let that happen to us, so I told most of the guys, especially those for guard duty that night, to be on guard when they might show up and give a signal if you hear anything, me included. We wanted to get even with them for the crappy treatment we had been enduring – a great way to do it without any backlash. As it happened, I was the one who heard some noise in the brush not too far from me, maybe 30 feet, so I signaled the other guards and yelled "Ok guys, let's get them men!" Let me tell you, you have never heard so much noise in the brush as the cadre were running for their lives! They knew what we might do if we captured them. Funny how the next day when we returned to our barracks the cadre never mentioned the incident, like it never happened. Guess we were not so dumb after all.

In another incident during Basic Training, I had been put on guard duty to circle a wooded area which had nothing else in it. After many laps I decided to take a break and stationed myself in the woods behind some trees near the guard shack. Pretty soon a jeep was coming with the Major and his driver. I waited a while as he looked around for me, then he let out with some cursing and "Where is that S.O.B. guard?". That's when I stepped out with my rifle raised and demanded, "Halt who goes there!" the standard comment, and made the Major and his driver toss their I.D. out so I could check it.

I played it as if it was for real. After I recognized them and saluted, the Major complimented me, ending that event.

I remember many soldiers complaining about the food. I know they start out with high quality meat and vegetables to cook with, but somehow mess it up. Well, what do you expect when they make a cook a mechanic and vice versa. Yes they really did that! It would seem to be true that there is a right way, a wrong way, and the Army way.

One evening we were having meat loaf, one of my favorites at home. When I tasted it, I no longer liked meat loaf. Somehow they managed to destroy it with the seasonings they used. Another dinner time they were really rushing me to eat fast, get outside and wait to march somewhere. I don't know why but that really pissed me off, so I took my time to eat my meal. An officer came in the mess hall to find me and see why I was not out with the rest of the guys. I told him I was not going to ruin my stomach by eating too fast and would you believe he agreed and waited for me to finish! There was no repercussions over that one either.

When you did K.P. (Kitchen Patrol) we worked about fifteen hours which is a longer day than when you are doing regular training. Glad I only had to do it once. Note: some things are too trivial to write about which no doubt would be boring.

I just remembered another event. (I call them events because it is out of the normal spectrum.) I just seem to have had a knack for embarrassing my superiors occasionally. As any veteran knows, there are daily inspections, only some are special as the one day when we really had to do a most thorough job. We were ready for the big brass inspection when I had a sudden attack to take a crap and could not wait for the inspection to be over. Perhaps not many people know that our toilets of today were invented by a man whose last name was Crapper which eventually replaced the outhouse. At first people would say "I am going to use the crapper", usual slang people come up with. Later, it was shortened to "I am going to take a crap." So now you know the rest of the story as to my use of that word and it does make the situation funnier, right? In the back of the barracks was the bathroom with six or more toilets out in the open, no privacy at all. Well there I was sitting on one of the crappers when the big brass walked in and it surprised them as I did my thing. They were a bit confused, not expecting this scenario I created but without further ado, they left. Never heard anything about that either.

Another thing we did during Basic Training was to go through a "combat course" with loaded M1A1 Carbine semi-automatic rifles. I had been looking forward to doing this course but was chosen to keep the records of what each man did instead. The course was about thirty or forty yards long, mostly mud with deep holes strategically placed at about six feet deep so some men being in the holes would hold up a stick with a target on it, raising it and lowering it for those going through the course to shoot at. Following that was a ten foot high wall of logs to climb over to complete the course. Well, when my buddy Richard Hensick went through the course, he set his Carbine on automatic and shot the targets off the stick. Then there were two guys, one black and one white, both with the same name, Henry Brown, who were the company screw ups. They went through the course at the same time (a coincidence), did not even hit one target and proceeded to climb the wall. About half way up, they slipped at the same time and fell backwards into the mud. They were like two peas in a pod! I wish I could have gotten a picture of that but my camera was stolen before I got to Fort Lee, Virginia for basic training.

Chapter III

ORDER CHANGE

After Basic Training there was eight more weeks of school to qualify us as "Quartermaster Unit Supply Specialist". Most of the time it was an instructor orating day after day, hot 90 degrees plus, and no air-conditioning. So it was extremely difficult to stay awake. We also had some reading to do, however I cannot say we learned very much. I was inducted on February 18th, 1952 so it was cold. When I got to Fort Lee, Virginia it was warmer but when we began school the temperature jumped into the nineties.

Before we were sent home on leave prior to going overseas, my company and two others that trained at the same time were slated to go to Japan for further training and then to Korea. About two weeks before going home on leave, I received a change in my orders sending me to the TRUST command in Trieste, Italy which is at the top of the "boot" separating Yugoslavia and Italy by the Adriatic Sea. TRUST stands for Trieste United States Troops. We bided our time at Camp Kilmer waiting for the ship that would take us to Trieste. While waiting, a friend of mine and I had an encounter.

Chapter IV

THE CHICKEN-SHIT CAPTAIN

One day while waiting at Camp Kilmer to go overseas, a friend and I were heading toward the gate to go off camp for the afternoon that weekend. About a block before the gate, a Chevy hardtop with a light blue and white paint job stopped beside us and a captain jumped out and started raking us over the coals for not saluting him. When in his car we could not see his rank, but this guy was what we call a "Chicken-Shit Officer". Next, he wanted to see our passes and kept them so we could not leave camp. After he left my buddy said he gave him a fake pass and still had his real one. I was not prepared for that and told my buddy I would meet him outside the camp and he should wait for me. What the Captain did not know was I just happened to be the company clerk in our section and went to the office, issued myself a new pass and rejoined my buddy outside the camp. Ha, ha to that jerk captain!

The next day I just happened to be in the office alone when that "Chicken-Shit Captain" called to complain about my not saluting. Well, I pretended to be a Major as company commander and reamed his ass out for wasting my time over that and hung up. He never called back. I have a great respect for authority but that jerk was over the top!

Chapter V

THE TRIP HOME ON LEAVE

After we graduated from school we were sent home by train for seventeen days leave (two days of travel). After arriving in Milwaukee I took a cab home. When someone answered the door no one seemed glad to see me, except for Ronnie, my youngest brother who was about six years old at the time. The first thing he did was recite all the commercials he had heard on TV. They knew I was coming home since I wrote a letter telling them. I did not write many letters home from Fort Lee, we didn't have much time to write. I could not believe the men who were homesick in basic training. I never was. I wanted to change into civilian clothes before going out anywhere. I found I had none. My folks gave them to my brother Bob. That made me feel like they were not expecting me home alive. Since that seemed to be the case I spent most of my time with friends and only returned home at night. My folks liked some shows on TV that did not interest me so when they went to bed I watched "Inner Sanctum" and then went to bed since that was when the station went off the air. It was a good show of the few that were on at that time. Channel 4 - that was it in 1952.

Going back, I had to take the train to

Chicago and transfer to another train to get to Camp Kilmer, New Jersey. My folks took me to the station in pa's 1934 Plymouth. My mother had tears in her eyes but I do not know about my dad. I would have liked to hug them but I was extremely shy and had seldom been shown much affection growing up. My dad told me years later that he could not show affection. I was puzzled about that because his mother was very affectionate, although grandpa was a bit gruff.

I had thought we would have been flown to Camp Kilmer which would be quicker than two days on a train. Camp Kilmer was a place of transition to going overseas or returning home.

Chapter VI

CAMP KILMER
SIGHT-SEEING

A few guys and I took a trip to New York City by train to check out "Greenwich Village" which we heard about. Unknowingly we entered a bar which turned out to be a gay bar (it wasn't called that then). We quickly departed that place and located a straight bar. There we met a man whom we asked if he would show us around the area. Then we would buy his drinks. He agreed, so onward we went. This was at night so we only saw the night life and it's true that this city never sleeps. We took the train to New York City again, but this time on the weekend during the day. It was far more interesting. We decided to visit the Empire State Building. Now I being from a fairly large city have been on some elevators, however this one had an operator and when we took off it went so fast I almost fell on the floor! If it was a car, like my 1968 Olds Toronado, it would have set you firm against your seat back. To go to the top, you had to take two different elevators, both fly like a rocket. We could see quite a bit of the city in every direction. The buildings were as far as you could see. After we left the Empire State Building, we went to Times Square. We were going to cross the street about two blocks from the Times Square building and quickly found ourselves committing suicide to try. Luckily, a person nearby told us we should go down some steps where there was a cover over them and a tunnel would take us to the other side of that street.

Next we visited Ellis Island where many, many people passed through to become Americans, including my mother's parents who came from Germany. When we were there it was a large room with a wooden floor and a crummy green paint job. I don't think they were using it anymore then. Lastly, we visited the 'Statue of Liberty'. We went all the way up to the crown of her head where you could observe out the windows and see the city, Manhattan Island, and the ships coming in and going out of port.

After we returned back to camp, we chose to use some of our free time to visit Richmond, Virginia a few times. We did a lot of walking and came across some girls who seemed interested in us. The one I talked to, we seemed to like each other, however, we soon learned their parents did not want us dating their girls. We were not good enough. Imagine that, here we are called up to fight and die for our country, but not good enough for their daughters! I guess some G.I.'s ruined it for the rest of us by using them and then dumping them when they got pregnant. Like the Navy, a girl in every port. I did not have a girlfriend back home, but that did not matter. Boo Hoo!

Chapter VII

THE JOHN W. GOTHELLS

At last we were escorted to the John W. Gothells troop ship to take us to our final destination of Trieste, Italy – but before getting there we had to make a few stops along the way. Our first stop was Naples, Italy. For what, I don't know. We did not stay long enough to take a tour. This city was where Sophia Loren was from. The buildings were built going up the side of hills, all made of some kind of concrete. They did have windows. Our second stop was Casablanca, Morocco. We were there long enough to take a tour. One thing we wanted to check out was the street where if you walk down it alone, you would disappear, never to be seen or heard from again! Since we were a large group we could safely walk down there. It did not seem any different from any other street. Of their buildings, they were something like concrete with no windows. The ground was mostly sand where we were. Next stop was Ankara, Turkey to deliver some military equipment. We docked right next to a Turkish troop ship loaded with their army troops. I noticed their skin was darker than ours. Neither we nor they spoke a common language so we found using a form of sign language worked. We kind of entertained each other that way until we left port for Athens, Greece. In Turkey, we were not allowed to go off ship on a tour and could not see much from the ship. In Athens we again were able to get off the ship and see a few of the sights there. We visited the Colosseum and other places I no longer remember what they were and then returned to our ship. Since I had my camera stolen from me back in the states, I could not take pictures to show what I had seen. Finally we were headed to Trieste. In all it took twenty-one days to get there from New York City. Normally it would take thirteen to fourteen days to get there direct.

Chapter VIII

LIFE ON THE OCEAN

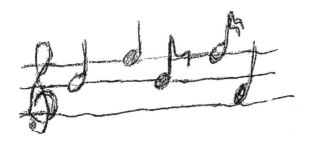

I bet you are wondering by now if anything had happened on our way across the ocean or if I may have forgotten. Well, the first day out, never having been on a ship before, I got seasick which lasted two days. The Navy 'chow' was great compared to Army 'chow'.

The first dumb thing that happened was

when our Master Sergeant decided we should have P.T. (physical training) each morning on deck. Well here we are, that is, the ship bobbing up and down like a cork on the Atlantic Ocean. After the first morning, the ship Captain said "Enough, no more P.T. because someone could get hurt and tossed overboard." That made the Sergeant look like a dumbbell.

A few days later, an officer, I think he was a First Lieutenant, was looking for someone to put together entertainment for the troops while on the ship. A fellow I knew told him I played the piano, so he found me and commandeered me to arrange something. I thought, what the hell do I know about putting on entertainment? I only play the piano! Well, in the service, when they tell you to do something, you do it even if you screw it up. I checked around and found four fellows who played the instrument I needed and of course we had no sheet music to use, just as it was when I was in Basic Training at the U.S.O. when a few of us had a jam session. At least this time we had some practice sessions together. During our practice time we seemed to meld together very well. It's a good thing we could play by ear (if you knew the melody we could fill in the rest). It seems we had to do two shows, first, one for the officers and then the rest of the troops. We did our best playing for about two hours for each and received great accolades from both. Mission accomplished. That pretty much covers the trip of anything worth mentioning.

Chapter IX

TRIESTE AT LAST

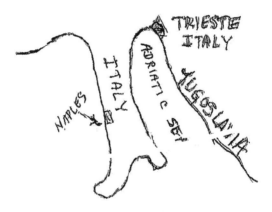

When we arrived in the port of Trieste, Italy, some of us were taken into the city where we were billeted in a hotel located in a plaza. A plaza is similar to a cul-de-sac here, except it is next to the main street and larger with a sculpture and fountain in the middle (six lanes wide of concrete) that goes through the middle of the city. The buildings of Trieste were all made of concrete if you can visualize that. No wooden structures at all. In the plaza, the street in that circle are large bricks. The edge of the partial circle has some stores, our billet and a street next to us that goes up the hill. About half a block up that street was where our P.T. space was and next to that was our motor pool.

After we were settled in and knew what our job would be, except in my case I was supposed to take over the Quartermaster supplies, but the Sergeant who was running it got another six months extension so I had to be placed elsewhere. I already had the classification of "Quartermaster Unit Supply Specialist". Now I had to be classified as an "Ordinance Unit Supply Specialist" which was done on the job because the two had enough similarities that I did not have to go back to school. Now I had two MOS's. As you will see as we go along in this story, I will acquire three more. Not the norm for a two year stint. As it was, they needed someone to handle the paperwork at the repair warehouse at the port. Repairs for things like trucks, tanks, trailers, etc.

We also learned that our company had their own nightclub where the G.I.'s could go after work and socialize. On some Fridays and/or Saturdays a band would come and play dance music. That was also when the girls showed up. One Friday when the band was there, I noticed an attractive girl was not dancing yet so I went over and asked her to dance with me. She did and some of the songs I knew the words to, so I sang to her a song or two. Later she excused herself to visit the ladies bathroom and must have told some of her girlfriends about my singing to her. Next thing I know, the girls were practically getting in line to dance with me so they could hear me sing. (In high school one of my majors was in music. I was a member of the chorus and in a few musicals put on by our music director. I also was a choir member in my church for many years.) I never imagined my voice was that good.

In retrospect, this area was the first hot spot after WWII as far as I know. In the past, Italy, Austria and Yugoslavia fought over this land. About half is mountains and farmland and the other half is the city of Trieste and industry. There formerly was British, French and American troops here to keep the peace. When I got there it was us and the British. Later, after I went home, they finally agreed that Italy would have Trieste and the industry and Yugoslavia would have the mountains and farmland.

Chapter X

My Encounter
with Miss Italy

On some weekends I would go on stage to play the piano. The music I played was not dance music. Well, one evening I was playing and a gorgeous young woman came in and all eyes at the bar were on her (about fifteen G.I.'s). They encircled her at the bar while having their beer. One of the guys came over to me, told me she was Miss Italy of 1950 or 1951 (I don't remember the exact year) and I should go over and join in. I said no thank you and continued playing. Soon she came over to me and asked why I did not come over. I said you seemed busy enough so I did not think you would even notice me. Well, after talking with her for a time, she asked if I would like to meet her for dinner at a nice restaurant the next day. I said sure, so we set a place and time to meet. Then she left our club. The next day I was where we were to meet, right on time. I waited and waited for about an hour and decided to leave. I guess her "no-show" was to spite me for not trotting over to her the prior night. Well, que sera, sera on that. I never saw her again – and so life goes on.

Chapter XI

ON THE JOB, FIRST OF MANY

Another odd thing that occurred one day, I came out of our billet to get my ride to work by truck but instead, here was a staff car and driver who said he was taking me to work now. I have one stripe, mind you, and I have a staff car and driver?! My job was paperwork to get repairs taken care of and released in our shop (things like tanks, trucks, trailers, etc.). This went on until I was needed to take over another job at "Issue Point" in a supply warehouse. Now here is the kicker, both jobs require at least a Sergeant and I am still a PFC, one stripe. I suspected the reason for the lack of promotion was because of rejecting going to O.C.S., why, because there was no other reason. I was able to do whatever job I was given well. Whenever we entered or left the gate at the port which was surrounded by a brick wall, the MP at the gate always saluted. I sometimes returned the salute but wondered if he was saluting me or the car. Normally a staff car is for officers only, you tell me why. I never found out why I had that convenience.

I had not worked there very long when an M46 tank which had a track repair was ready to be released but had to be road-tested first. I learned that I was to take it out for a test run. I never drove a tank before and I protested. Nothing to it, I was told, and someone showed me where to start it and engage the transmission. There were two levers to operate the tracks for steering. The Master Sergeant said to test it by going full-speed down this dirt street between warehouses and when you reach the building that's in your way, slam on the brakes and engage one track so it spins the tank around a few times. If the repaired track holds, it's ready to release from the shop. Well, that was an experience. I thought later, what would happen if the track broke again, then what would the tank do? Glad I didn't have to find out!

Chapter XII

Colonel and Lady – Mascot Dogs

Our company, it seems, had two mascots. Colonel was the name of the white male dog who weighed about forty pounds. He was born in a tank during WWII in a battle zone. Because of this and being in a war zone for some time, the dog was given an official rank of Colonel, thus his name as well. I don't have the rest of his story but Colonel wound up in our billet (Ordinance Supply). Somewhere along the way, before I came to Trieste, Lady was acquired. No one seemed to know where she came from, however the two dogs became one, like they were married, and went everywhere together. Lady was a different breed from Colonel. She was a small dog, short legs, brown and white with a little black in color, a little chunky and weighed about twenty pounds. They were very friendly dogs.

Here is where it gets funny. Well, since the dogs were not fixed eventually Lady was in heat and when they were out and around other dogs were trying to jump her and Colonel fought them off. For some reason, Colonel could not jump her for a few days but finally was able to. That day, they were locked together and found their way into the café behind our billet on a cross street. Somehow when Colonel was locked in her, he managed to rotate around so they were back to back and Colonel led the way into the café. A waitress squirted them with water thinking that might separate them. It did not work and everyone was laughing during this event. You just have to wait until they are ready to separate. She had three puppies who looked exactly like Colonel. Two were born dead while only one survived. Believe it or not, she ate the dead puppies! I never saw anything like that before. After a few weeks the surviving puppy disappeared. I guess someone took him home.

Another event concerning Colonel was about a certain Sergeant who took care of their food and water. Well, occasionally he would come back to our billet drunk. One of these times he had a bottle of beer in his hand and poured the beer into Colonel's water bowl and Colonel lapped it up with gusto! After emptying the bowl, Colonel proceeded to walk away and was slipping and stumbling all over, finally going somewhere and barfing up the beer. He then seemed to be sober again. That dog sure liked his beer!

Chapter XIII

GUARD DUTY?

One evening when I was going out we had
a nineteen year old R.A. on duty who let his

authority get carried away. In order to leave our billet when off duty, we had to sign out (name and time). There was a desk near the door, a sign out sheet and an armed guard sitting there. After I signed out and was heading to the door he told me I can't leave unless I take the kit if I'm planning to have sex with a prostitute – not his authority. He threatened to shoot me if I did not take the kit even though I told him I was not going out for sex. I told him he better not miss because if he did I would take that rifle from him, shove it up his ass and pull the trigger! He did nothing. Give some guys a little power and they abuse it, like that "Chicken-Shit Captain". By the way, an R.A. (Regular Army) is a guy who enlisted and we draftees called them "Royal Assholes".

Chapter XIV

CONFLICTS AND SHORT JOBS

One day a Master Sergeant had a beef with me, I don't really recall what it was and he said I could not get a job in civilian life and that was why I was in the Army. Mind you, I was drafted, not enlisted, and had to leave my civilian job which wasn't much of a job at that time. I told him I thought that was why he was in the Army because he could not get a job in civilian life. Then he left. There were other incidents like that, even a fight, but not enough there to write about.

One morning we had to go down to a ship

that came in with military supplies such as trucks of a different size and other items. One truck we unloaded was an REO two and a half ton which was to replace the GMC's from WWII and possibly earlier. The GMC's you had to double-shift to change gears and you needed pretty good arm muscle in order to steer it. The REO's were easy to steer, power steering and you could even shift without using the clutch if you rev the engine to the right level. It had power breaks also.

I had a few short-term jobs before I began my permanent one. One was Company Clerk for a few months, another was K.P. for a day, driving the truck to transport food for our company. The last one I remember was driving a First Lieutenant around in a jeep. His former driver went home and I took over temporarily until a permanent one showed up. One day we drove up to the castle where our commanding general was living. To my surprise, I got to meet him while there. He was short of stature and reminded me of my Grandpa Wells, except Grandpa was six feet tall.

One job that I acquired while doing my regular job was as a Physical Training instructor which we had every morning before going to work. Later they gave it to someone trained in that area.

Chapter XV

COMMUNISTS CAME TO TRIESTE

Finally after waiting for the guy I would replace to go home, I took over my permanent assignment as "Ordinance Equipment Repair Specialist". I called it "paper clerk" to process repairs and releases, some requiring tests before release. This became my third M.O.S. I settled in and acquainted myself with the paperwork and moved forward. I already spoke of some experiences on this job (the 1946 tank and the use of the staff car, a 1952 Chevy).

I had gone to work one morning when I noticed just before going through the gate, something unusual. The train depot is close to the gate wall and a large number of people were exiting the train, heading for the main street that goes through the middle of Trieste. After work I returned to my billet to find I had a problem. There were a thousand or more people on the main street demonstrating for something, causing trouble. The VG police (civilian) which were trained by U.S. MP's were shooting their weapons over the heads of these people who turned out to be communists. The buildings as I explained earlier, were made of thick concrete (24") and bullets were ricocheting all over the place, numerous bullets coming very close to me and the other two guys watching with me outside our billet. That was dumb of us and we retracted to inside the billet where it was a little safer. No sense in becoming an unintended casualty.

When you want to stay in your billet and relax, your superiors can't leave you alone – for some stupid reason they have to put you to work doing something. I hated that, so one evening around 6:30 PM I decided to see a movie at the American theater only to find I had already seen that movie. Now here is where it gets weird. I decided to go to the British theater, thinking to see a movie I had not seen there, the only other English speaking theater. I proceeded to walk down to the main drag where the demonstrators were, six lanes wide and without thinking it could be dangerous I continued down the sidewalk and the crowd opened a pathway for me to go through all the way (about six blocks) to the cross street where the British theater was. It was like Moses parting the Red Sea! The theater was about one block up the side street and when I arrived, the front was smashed and the theater closed. I was disappointed and began the trek back through the crowd, again opening a pathway for my return to my company billet or the café behind our billet on a back street. Mind you, I walked through that crowd about six blocks to return to my quarters. The whole time I never gave a thought to it being dangerous during that trek and I can't explain that.

What was even stranger was what some fellows who watched me go through that crowd and return unscathed said when I mentioned the trek. They said there were three giant men following right behind me the entire trip and that's why they opened a pathway for me. I believe they were angels because I never saw them.

Chapter XVI

THE GENERAL

Now the rest of the story. After a few days of discontent our General had enough of it. Hold on, I am a little bit ahead of myself. I don't want to forget an important part of this story. The rioters had taken down the American flag from the Mayor's office, the official flag at that time and replaced it with the Italian flag. A British company of men came marching down the street to the Mayor's office, took down the Italian flag and raised the American flag back up and told them not to do that again. After the British left, they took it down again and put up the Italian flag. This time a company of American troops led by a Colonel marched to the Mayor's office, removed the Italian flag and returned our flag to the pole. Then the Colonel told these communists, "If you do that again, we will shoot your ass off!" No more problem.

Finally the General announced over the radio, "If you don't live here in Trieste, leave by 4:00 P.M. today or I will declare Martial Law." and that would be their end. Before 4:00 P.M. we were organized into riot squads with loaded M1's and bayonets to make sure they left. I was observing the nervous reaction of some of the guys; I saw one guy just talk and talk, another was fidgeting a lot, another was as quiet as a mouse, etc. – for me, I seemed to be elated. I had to go down to the warehouse before this was over and as I was passing the train station, you would not believe how packed with people it was, trying to get out of Dodge, fast. They were practically climbing over each other to get out. That was the end of that problem.

Chapter *XVII*

THE BOYS

When I had been in my ordinance company for a few weeks I learned where noncommissioned G.I.'s went after work. They had a bar where all they did was drink beer, cuss a lot and roll in the sack with prostitutes. I did not seem to fit in there.

Later I learned about the U.S.O. club and found their music room where a piano was waiting for me to play it. After playing it for a while (and thank goodness it was in tune) three young fellows came in and asked if they could stay and listen to me play. Eventually they introduced themselves – first was Bob (Umberto) a seventeen year old Italian high school student, next was Peter the son of a Colonel, and last was Richard the son of a Sergeant, all seventeen years old. One thing Bob asked me to do was help him get rid of his accent even though he already spoke very good English, but I did complete his transition. He wanted to be as American as much as he could because he was going to be sponsored by an uncle in the states so he could be an American. Unfortunately, I lost track of him when I went home, so I don't know if he got here, nor where he might be. He would be 84 this year. I learned his dad was a ship Captain and the last few years he would take new ones out for a shakedown run. I met his family when he invited me to dinner at his home. It was an apartment in one of those all-concrete buildings. They did not have a furnace or fireplace in their home. The temperature was pretty constant in their apartment any day, night or weather change. He had a sister about eight years old. Bob told me his dad wanted me to say something in Italian. They seemed pleased with my pronunciation of the words. When you learn to speak Italian, you must remember their vowels. For example, our "a" is "ah", "e" is "i" and "o" is "ou", there is no "u".

One day Peter invited me to his home for dinner and his house was the only wood frame home in that area. It was up on a hill where the view was covering miles of terrain. The Colonel was not there that day at dinner so I don't know if I ever met him.

Chapter XVIII

YUGOSLAVIA

Moving on to the summer of 1953, Bob Peter, Richard and I were discussing what we would do that evening. Bob, who seemed to be the other boys' leader, said "Why don't we go into Yugoslavia to a tavern owned by a friend of his and have a party?" I said it sounded like fun except if I got caught there I could get twenty years in prison and who knows what would happen to Peter and Richard. Bob said he would have three of his friends go with us. It will be arranged for a watch to be set up to keep an eye out for the communist guards that patrol the mountainous area. Bob also said the Yugoslavian people like Americans and would make sure we would not be caught. If we were it would have been an embarrassment for the U.S. government too. I was twenty-two years old at the time and all the others were seventeen – high school students. We decided to go, regardless of the risk.

That evening, after dusk, we proceeded carefully, taking side streets and darkened areas on our trek out of Trieste to the pathway up the mountains, a narrow path to our destination. Along the way, which was an hour walk, we encountered a patrol, but they did not see us as we ducked out of sight. We proceeded after they were out of sight to the bar. It was dark outside by the time we got there. We went in and were given a very friendly greeting even though the bartender did not speak much English. We sat down at a large round table, all eight of us around it. The bar there is very unique compared to American bars. Each of us were given a shot of an orange liqueur. Then we had to sing a song together and if you flub a word you have to down the shot and it's refilled. I probably flubbed more than anyone else. Although, by the time we ended the game everyone was feeling their oats. To this day, I do not remember anything after we walked out of the bar to return to Trieste. My friends made sure I got back to my billet safely. By that time I had sobered up pretty well. That orange liqueur was pretty tasty so when I returned to the states I wanted to buy a bottle but no one had any. That excursion is one I will never forget.

Chapter XIX

MY RIFLE?

One day in the summer of 1953 we were going on bivouac and camped out for two days and nights. We had pup tents to set up which were very small. We had no padding to lie on, just the rocky ground. Needless to say, I could not sleep on the ground so since I drove one of the trucks bringing men to the bivouac area, a two-and-one-half ton truck, I climbed into it and slept on the nice cushioned seat with my rifle on the floor. The next morning we were suddenly awakened and told to assemble to attack a small town not far away and secure it. Well, I hurried out to join the rest of the troops and in my rush, forgot my rifle. In the process of the attack a Sergeant asked me where my rifle was. I said back in my truck and he said to go back and get it. Well, by the time I did, it was too late, the battle was over, and the troops had captured the town. Since I seldom carried a weapon, it's understandable how I left it behind, however in real combat I could have been killed. Never again, I vowed, would I forget my weapon.

Chapter XX

THE CAFÉ

I spoke earlier about a café behind our billet facing a street there – just around the corner from our billet. Shortly after entering Trieste, I learned of this café so I went there to check it out. For the first time I tried their Italian coffee. It was in a tiny cup which might have held two ounces max. I liked the coffee which was sweet to the taste. Never add anything to it. Next I decided to try their ham and pickled pepper sandwich, it was delicious. After that experience

I would frequently go there just before hitting the sack for an evening snack. This café was the same one our mascots (the two dogs) frequented and had their "locked together" encounter.

Chapter *XXI*

THE ACCIDENT

One evening I was standing outside the U.S.O. club enjoying a nice warm night and looking toward the canal which ran through part of the city of Trieste fairly close to the Adriatic Sea. In front of me there was a three-lanes-wide street with a bridge crossing the canal. There were walls on each side of the canal to prevent erosion. While looking across the street where the bridge was, a British one-and-a-half ton truck was coming from the right of me and I noticed a dog jumped out of the rear of the truck and the soldiers' truck was veering to the right, going up on the sidewalk where an older couple were walking hand-in-hand. The truck hit the man from the back, flipped him up in the air and dropped him into the canal; killing him instantly! The American MP's showed up and were trying to find witnesses that saw what happened. I told them I saw the event and seemed to be the only person who did. They asked a lot of questions, took my name, rank and where I was billeted, then I went on my way.

A few days later I was summoned to an interrogation by the Army's equivalent of the C.I.A. I guess to see if I had any grudge against the Brits, mind you, my last name is Wells, an English name and part of my ancestry, so why would I have any animosity toward them? Well, I was certified then to testify. A few weeks later I was summoned to appear before a British court (the judge was a Major) to testify about what I saw. The Major addressed me as private and I corrected him by saying "PFC". His reply was "Oh, you Americans." I guess he was annoyed with that. So I could show them exactly what happened, they had a small board with the street, canal, bridge, sidewalk and a truck so I could move the truck the way I saw it go. The judge said "Are you sure the direction the truck took?" "Yes", I said. I cannot imagine what difference it would make, the way the truck was going, it still killed the man. Then a recess was called because it was tea time. I was taken to a room where the truck driver was and we drank tea together and talked. I wouldn't be surprised if they wire-tapped to see what we said. I did not even like tea but I drank it anyway to be polite. I believe they decided against a Court Martial and I was sent back to my billet. As far as I was concerned, the dog caused the accident when he distracted the driver. And so goes another event biting the dust.

Chapter XXII

THE GIRLFRIEND

Normally in Trieste the G.I.'s would mostly see prostitutes soliciting, but sometimes one can get lucky. I was outside the U.S.O. club in the daytime on the weekend and saw an attractive young blond woman wearing no makeup at all, walking by. I smiled and she smiled back so I started some conversation with her. She spoke very good English and we seemed to hit it off very well. We walked around the city and talked quite a bit. She said she was from a small village on one of the hills around Trieste. Unfortunately, I don't remember the name of her village nor her name either. Eventually we wound up at the café behind my billet to have some food. We really hit it off very well and dated frequently. One evening she said I could walk her home. When we reached her village there were hecklers insulting her and made some comment about me, in Italian of course. I moved toward them like I was going to chase them and they reacted by backing off and stopped the insults. She said it was probably best I don't walk her all the way to her home so from there I kissed her and left. At some point, we decided we wanted to get married. Well, in order to make that happen, we had to make an appointment to see the chaplain. He interviewed us and said he would have to do a background check on her. Well, it seems there was someone in her family who had cancer and died. This meant she was rejected to be my wife. After learning that, she just disappeared and I never saw her again; not my choice. A few weeks later I was in the American theater for a movie and in walks the chaplain and stopped to say hello. He asked me how my girlfriend was and I told him, "Gone, and I never saw her again." I was in tears over that. He said he was sorry to hear that. Then the movie started and he sat down a few rows away from me. And so goes a love lost that was a might-have-been.

Chapter XXIII

OFFICER VS. ENLISTED

There were two incidents that occurred you might find of interest. They happened a few weeks apart. The first one was an enlisted man whose father was dying and you had to ask the Red Cross to get transportation home for emergencies. Well, he was turned down. Along came the second one, an officer, whose father was having a minor operation. Zip, he was flown home immediately! We who knew of these incidents vowed we would never again give any money to the RED CROSS. Also, at that time when the Red Cross was called in for some emergency they doled out stale doughnuts and rotten tasting coffee. Maybe they have changed since then, but anytime their name comes up, we remember what they did and the anger returns. I bet you may know someone who can tell you about the Red Cross back then. Some clergy preach to forgive, but the Bible says if they repent you are to forgive.

Chapter XXIV

TOUGH GUYS

If I may regress back to when I first came to Trieste. Sometimes my memory comes back about events not necessarily in the order they occurred. This is about two tough guys. When I was assigned a room in our company's hotel, it just had to be the room where two tough guys were. My bunk was across the room from them, about five feet of space. The Corporal was a good-looking muscular guy about 5'6" tall and his buddy looked like a mob hit man, a little chubby and maybe 5'3" tall. Well, one evening those two went out and later some G.I.'s who had seen what happened, told me about it. It seems while they were walking down a street minding their own business, seven Italian men going by across the street began heckling them and insulting them in Italian. Well, it so happens the Corporal and his buddy understood what they said and replied with some insulting things back. That's when these seven guys came running over to them to beat up the Corporal and his buddy. Well, it went the other way. The Corporal and his buddy beat the crap out of those seven Italians. When the boys returned there was not a scratch on them nor soiled clothes. They never said anything about their encounter. I know I would not want to tangle with them.

Chapter XXV

TRANSFER TO ORDINANCE SUPPLY WAREHOUSE

They needed someone to take over "Issue Point" since the guy doing that job was going home. I was appointed to take over that job, so I was transferred. Always paperwork. And again, this job required a Sergeant to run it. As before, here I am still a "lowly" PFC, one stripe. I don't know how they got away with that. Well, not long after, maybe a few months into the job, another event was to occur, not a normal one. The Captain and his First Sergeant had received a "TDY" (special assignment) for two to three months and would not be around to do their job (both of them). Yes, they appointed me to take over running the warehouse while they were gone. Now isn't that funny? Here I am, a lowly PFC and I am supposed to do both the Captain's job and his First Sergeant's job! There were about twenty G.I.'s under me, most of whom outranked me and yet not one of them objected to taking orders from me. Thank God, I must have done something right! I also had a dozen civilian Italians under me. Only one, Louie, spoke English so I gave him orders to direct what his men should do.

There also was an American civilian who worked with me to coordinate unloading the ships when they came into port and making sure his invoice covered everything we were to receive. When new trucks of different sizes were unloaded, I thought they would return the old equipment back to the states. I was told they dumped it into the Adriatic Sea because it was cheaper than sending those vehicles home. The only thing they kept were the jeeps which were rebuilt and sold to Italian civilians cheap. We were not allowed to buy one and send it home. Talk about polluting the waters!

Chapter XXVI

CROSS COUNTRY RACE

One weekend I had heard there was to be a car race from Trieste starting near our billet and going up the hill to a town called Sistana, a winding road up a low mountain. The cars would be timed on how long it took them to get there. The race started with the most powerful car first, down to the last car, a Fiat two-seater. The first car, a Ferrari, was doing 80 mph in about two blocks. There were other cars such as a BMW and a number of others with lower horse-power capability until the last car, the Fiat two-seater. Well, the Fiat was revving up his engine and shifting from one gear to the next and barely moving. I could have walked faster than he was going! Those two cars were the ones to stand out, however, the others were fairly fast too, but not like the first and not as slow the last one. I think the run was about two miles long. After seeing that race I thought the Ferrari was the car I would buy when I returned home, until I found they were priced at $80,000 at that time. My civilian job at that time paid less than a dollar an hour. At that rate it would, if I saved every penny, take about 356 years to get that amount together! We know who won the race, but I always wondered if the Fiat ever finished the race.

Chapter *XXVII*

THE COLONEL'S DAUGHTER

I don't recall where I met the Colonel's daughter but I think it may have been at a dance, perhaps at our nightclub. Anyway, we hit it off pretty well and I walked her home where she lived with her dad. She invited me in for a while, we talked, we kissed, and then I had to return to my billet. (Bet you thought there was more.) Her dad was not there and the temptation was strong, but her having her period ended that. Later, when her father returned home, he wanted to know if we did anything and she said no and the reason.

I learned she had another boyfriend she

dumped, but he thought she belonged to him. He was very possessive and even threatened her dad. I was surprised he wasn't court-martialed for that. He turned out to be a Section 8 (a loony-toon) and somehow had found out about me, called me on the phone at my billet and threatened to kill me! He actually wanted me to come to where he was to do it! I said 'no', if you want to kill me, you will have to come where I am. He was a no-show. I checked up on him since he said his name. It seems he was in Korea before being sent to Trieste and he supposedly dropped onto a grenade to save his platoon leader and received a medal for it. He has been off-the-wall ever since and I don't know why they did not send him home, rather than here in Trieste. After he had threatened me they did send him home. I did not see her again for some time because I was sent to NCO school which is in a secluded area just on a small beach area of the Adriatic Sea. As soon as I went to NCO school I was promoted to PFC, one stripe.

They have tours there for anyone who wants to come because there is a cutout and partial cave where the Germans had a gun emplacement in case the U.S. would attack there during WWII. I happened to be on guard duty in the tunnel when a tour group showed up and there she was. As soon as she saw me she came running to me and wrapped her arms around me, making me uncomfortable because when you're on guard duty you can't have a woman groping you. I told her my situation and that she will get me in trouble. Finally she left with the group and I never saw her again. The timing was bad to work that out.

Chapter XXVIII

New Year's Eve Party

I know laws in Italy are somewhat different than in the States, so I thought, since I had uninhibited access to the Officers Club, I would take my three friends for a treat on New Year's Eve. That would be Bob, Pete and Richard who I mentioned earlier in this story. We assembled around 7:00 P.M. and entered the officers club around 8:00 P.M. I went to the bar and ordered two bottles of champagne and four glasses. We sat at a small, round table and began serving up the drinks. Bob and I had one bottle. Pete and Richard had the other. I noticed there were hardly any people in the club besides us. Perhaps the officers had home parties. I am not sure. We had a good time together and had a snoot-full that night. While going back to my billet with my friends, an MP in a jeep stopped and asked if I was going to make it back to my billet and offered me a ride. I said I needed to walk off the booze and could make it on my own. I thanked him for the offer.

Chapter XXIX

THE LAST JOB

I was transferred one more time to what is called G2. This is where all the big brass are from day to day. When I entered their forum I was saluting like crazy, remember, I was still a PFC, but they told me to knock off the saluting in here. Apparently they were very informal there. The First Sergeant there greeted me when joining their group and said the first thing he wanted to do was promote me to Corporal. I thanked him for the offer but said, why bother, I was going home in two months and he says, well, at least it's more money. I said I was supposed to be an

SFC (5 stripes) by now and if the Army thinks I will reenlist after being short-changed on rank, they have another guess coming. I know I did a superior job at every one they gave me so I am satisfied with that even though I was denied promotions without legitimate cause.

Chapter XXX

REAL CHEFS

A mini story to be sure and if you remember what I said about the cooks, I had two months before I was to return to the states. Two young men came to our company who were actually chefs in civilian life and were sons of chefs. When they took over the mess we ate like kings from then on. Instead of the usual slop, the morning our chefs began cooking, we entered the mess hall and each individual was asked what they wanted for breakfast and received it. Imagine that, to be given gourmet food to order, starting with breakfast. I enjoyed their cooking until I had to go home.

Chapter XXXI

Court Martial?

Another shorty, which seems important enough to mention. I was to appear before several officers for a possible court martial? I was confused. The room was dark that I entered. I knew we did have electricity. I was told I had disobeyed a direct order from my boss, a Master Sergeant, a nice guy. Since he was there, even though I could not see him, I said, "Have I ever disobeyed any order before?" He said, "No." I said, "Then why would I do that now?" Never did find out what order I disobeyed and I guess they decided to drop it.

Chapter *XXXII*

Something Overlooked

I did not mention that earlier in Trieste when I had hurt my back lifting too much weight, the neck on a large trailer to hook up to a truck. I was pretty strong, but I'm afraid two of us should have lifted it. Although I did not feel it right away, the next morning I could not get out of bed. Well, if you recall I spoke of a tough guy Corporal who demanded I get up. I was in the upper bunk and rolled out, falling on the floor. Then the dummy realized I was not faking my strained back. I was taken on sick-call to see a doctor. By then I was able to move slowly.

The doctor told me not to lift anything heavy for a while. So guess what? After returning to Camp Kilmer we would be given some duties while awaiting our orders to go home. I told this Sergeant I was told not to do any heavy lifting, so what does he do - puts me on unloading duffle bags from train cars. Okay, I thought to myself, you want to play dirty, so can I.

Before the next morning at roll call I acquired a clipboard, paper and pencil, also two men to follow me around. After roll call the next day, we slipped away and began my plan. Officers have a way of standing tall and walking in a confident manner which I emulated. The three of us, my cohorts walking a little behind me, went all over the camp. No one would engage us because they thought we were the Army's version of the C.I.A. Since no rank was showing other than my one stripe, they must have assumed I was high-ranking. That took care of the Sergeant's ignorance and I believe you have to be a leader to pull that off.

Chapter *XXXIII*

ONE MORE THING

Just when I thought I have recalled everything, I remembered something else you might find amusing. At some point in my "vacation" in Trieste, my company commander, a Captain summoned me to his office about something and my reply was, "I was born to lead, not follow." I don't know what possessed me to say that, but the captain chuckled at that. I left his office and went back to my job. The next day I learned I was to assemble the company and march them around for some practice. Well, I did it and as I suspected, a few guys were going to goof off which would make me look bad. The guys knew me as an easy-going guy but they quickly responded to my saying, "And if anyone goofs off to make me look bad, plan on dropping down to do twenty pushups!" That inspired those two goofs to snap to it and I was pleased to say, "I bet the captain didn't think I could do it."

Chapter XXXIV

Bye, Bye Trieste

I really enjoyed my stay in Trieste. I am no longer the shy guy I was. I had many good times and strange events but now it was time to go home. After securing my gear (duffle bag) with everything in it, I was taken by truck with a few other guys to board the ship home. Now even if we were passengers on the ship, there always seemed to be chores to do. Well, wouldn't you know, even though I am still a PFC, I was put in charge of guys to do the work. Other than that, there was not much going on worth mentioning on the trip to New York, U.S.A. When nearing port I asked to go topside so I could see the "Statue of Liberty" but no one was allowed as we entered port. When we got off the ship an Army truck took us to Camp Kilmer. We were deposited in a barracks where we would stay until we received our mustering-out papers.

Chapter XXXV

THE FINAL CALL

Every morning we have roll call, then after lunch they have another one where the names of everyone to head for home that day is called. I listened and wouldn't you know it, my name was not called even though I thought it should. After he was done I went up and said I did not hear my name called. He looked at his list and sure enough my name was there. I would hate to think what would happen if I had not asked. The sooner the better to get out of there. After receiving my orders I was taken to Grand Central Station in New York City and, by train, headed to Chicago, Illinois. From there I took a train which ran from Chicago to Milwaukee and back again. From Milwaukee I took a cab home. And then there could be another story?

One final thing happened after I had been home for some time. I saw a movie starring Robert Mitchum where he had the same type of clipboard that I had. What a coincidence. I tried to check to find out the movie name and what year it was made. No luck.

Well, this is the end of this story – to be continued?

Printed in the United States
By Bookmasters